D Y N A M I T E

Winner of the 2015 Frost Place Chapbook Competition

DYNAMITE

poems by

ANDERS CARLSON-WEE

BULL★CITY PRESS

DURHAM, NORTH CAROLINA

DYNAMITE

Winner of the 2015 Frost Place Chapbook Competition
Selected by Jennifer Grotz

Published in the United States of America

Library of Congress Cataloging-in-Publication Data

Carlson-Wee, Anders
Dynamite: poems / by Anders Carlson-Wee
p.   cm.
ISBN-13: 978-1-4243-1804-9

Book design by Flying Hand Studio

Published by
BULL CITY PRESS
1217 Odyssey Drive
Durham, NC 27713

www.BullCityPress.com

ACKNOWLEDGMENTS

The author would like to thank the editors of the following journals, in which these poems first appeared:

Best New Poets 2012: "Northern Corn"

Blackbird: "Birdcalls," "The Raft," "Flood of '97"

Forklift, Ohio: "Living"

Linebreak: "Clausen's Dog"

New Delta Review: "Riding the Owl's Eye"

New England Review: "Shoalwater"

Ninth Letter: "Dynamite," "The Low Passions"

Ninth Letter Online: "Volunteer"

The Journal: "Gathering Firewood on Tinpan"

The Missouri Review: "Butte," "Moorcroft," "County 19," "Listening to a Rail in Mandan"

The Paris-American: "Polaroid"

The Pinch: "Icefisher"

West Branch: "To the Fingerless Man in Banff"

"Icefisher" also appeared in *Best New Poets 2014* and *LitRagger*

"Northern Corn" also appeared in *LitRagger*

Thanks to the National Endowment for the Arts, the Camargo Foundation, the Dorothy Sargent Rosenberg Poetry Foundation, the Board of Trustees of The Frost Place, the Creative Writing Program at Vanderbilt University, Fairhaven College, the Sewanee Writers' Conference, and the Bread Loaf Writers' Conference for valuable funding and support.

Many thanks to Jennifer Grotz, Ross White, B.H. Fairchild, Traci Brimhall, Mary Cornish, Bruce Beasley, Claudia Emerson, Mark Jarman, Rick Hilles, Beth Bachmann, Kate Daniels, Oliver de la Paz, A. Van Jordan, Rick Barot, Jessica Faust, Speer Morgan, Stan Tag, Brandon Courtney, W.S. Lyon, Simone Wolff, Alicia Brandewie, Daniel Haney, Max McDonough, and Mary Somerville.

Special thanks to Kai Carlson-Wee and Edgar Kunz.

CONTENTS

DYNAMITE

My brother hits me hard with a stick
so I whip a choke-chain

across his face. We're playing
a game called *Dynamite*

where everything you throw
is a stick of dynamite,

unless it's pine. Pine sticks
are rifles and pinecones are grenades,

but everything else is dynamite.
I run down the driveway

and back behind the garage
where we keep the leopard frogs

in buckets of water
with logs and rock islands.

When he comes around the corner
the blood is pouring

out of his nose and down his neck
and he has a hammer in his hand.

I pick up his favorite frog
and say If you come any closer

I'll squeeze. He tells me I won't.
He starts coming closer.

I say a hammer isn't dynamite.
He reminds me that everything is dynamite.

RIDING THE OWL'S EYE

Out of all the dumpsters that could have been
empty, all the weather that could have bloomed
over the prairie and ruined me, all the cars
that could have sped by without hesitating and left me
on the fog-line nameless forever. The trains
that could have taken my legs. The hobos
that could have pulled a switchblade and opened me
like a flood enfolding the red North Dakota clay.
Out of all the hazards we pass through
in amazement, all the stories we tell of luck
and good fortune and prayer and survival, it is always
our own lungs that dry up and darken,
our own miles that straighten, our own hunger
that wanes. The Lord gives us mountains
and we fail to mine out that grandness.
The Lord gives us trains and we waste those distances
transporting coal. Some say the world is broken,
some say the Good Lord has forsaken our dreams,
but I say it is our own throat that grows
the cancer, our own asthma that blackens our breath
to a wheeze. And the truth is, the mile-long train
will always crawl past. The socket-fixed gaze
of the owl's skull will always turn perfectly
backwards. We will always be bodies among ghosts.
And what is important to them is not how we ride
on the westbound freighter, not how we shiver,
not how we crawl crooked and thin
and climb yet again into the trembling eye-hole.
It is not about suffering. It is not about fear.
We must peer out from inside the owl's eye.

Watch the coal-dust cook in the wind-eddies.
Watch it linger. Watch it spiral thinly as it bruises
the blue-faded mind of the buffalo sky.
We must be the pupil that swells in the coming darkness.
The cargo worth carrying across the distances.

BIRDCALLS

I crept around the dark train yard
while my brother watched for bulls.
Two days deep into the Badlands
and all our water gone. We had a birdcall
for if you saw something and another
for if you heard. A silent yard eight strings wide
with a few junkers parked. The horizon
a dull burn. The rails lit dimly by dew.
I was looking for the water bottles
the conductors used and threw out the windows
with maybe a sip left inside them.
I found one by stepping on it.
I sucked it like a leech. I stumbled
up and down the ballast and found five more,
unbuttoning my shirt and nesting them
against my chest upright and capless.
We had the sandpiper for if you should run
and the flycatcher for if you should hide.
I can't remember why we had the loon.
I crouched in the space between coal trains,
cradling the bottles and feeling the weight
of how little I had to spill.
I rubbed coal on my face. I felt crazy.
I thought about being found like this.
I tried to imagine what my story would be.
A version with my brother in it.
A version with no brother. I swear
I could smell rain a thousand miles away.
I could smell rain in the soot. I folded my hands
around my lips and made the gray ghost,
which told him where I was.
And also meant stay alert.
And also meant some other things
only owls understood.

VOLUNTEER

For a couple years I volunteered
at the prosthetics center in the south wing
of St. Mary's Memorial. Every Thursday
I pushed the lab equipment up against
the walls, mopped the floor, moved it back.
I was basically a janitor, but they called me
a *Lab Assistant*, trying to make it
sound important. All the patients who
came in were missing something.
Usually an arm or a leg. A clean loss.
A stub that still moved. The kind of thing
you would think of. But other times
it wasn't. This one guy had skin
where his nostrils should be. A fire maybe.
This girl was missing three fingers and part
of her palm. Probably an accident
with a handgun, but she was so young.
I would mop the floor and try to guess
what had happened to everyone. Watch
as they practiced walking across the room
with silicone toes. Listen carefully
as they dropped spoons on the clean floor
from experimental hands.

NORTHERN CORN

Traveling alone through Minnesota
as the corn comes in. Steel silos filling
to the brim. Black trees leaning
off the south sides of hills as the cold light
falls slantwise against the gristmills.
You have allowed another year to pass.
You have learned very little.
But that little is what you are throwing
in the furnace. That little is stoking the dust-
coals of last year and burning something.
Burning blue. The ninety-year-old father
is bringing his crop in. He climbs
off the thresher, checks the engine,
moves an oak branch. He pours
rye whiskey from a thermos and sips
the lidless excess of his private noon.
The size of his hands. The size of one finger.
The flathead prairie of his calloused
thumb-pad. He lies awake in the middle
of the night and whispers something
and suddenly loves his son again.
The way excess falls through him.
The way oil runs down the Mississippi River
and remains on the surface and burns.
The father no longer breathing.
The respirator breathing. The father lying
in a hospital bed in a nightgown.
The plastic tubes and machinery.
The whole hospital breathing.
The janitor waxing the white-tile floors
at midnight while life is trying hard
to leave. You must go to your father

while he is still your father.
You must hold him. You must kiss him.
You must listen. You must see the son
in the father and wonder. You must admit
that you wonder. Stand above him
and wonder. Drop his swelled-up hand.
Whisper something. Now unplug the machine.

CLAUSEN'S DOG

We float the rubber lifeboat down the cul-de-sacs.
Through the backyards of pre-fabs and ramblers
where the tops of small trees beckon
like oil-blackened hands. We are looking
for animals. Dogs and cats and other pets left behind
because leaving them behind was the rule
during the evacuation. For hours there is nothing.
Silence and the sculling of a plastic paddle.
The far-off gas station sunken past the pumps.
The hundred-year flood covering everything
three feet deep. When we find Clausen's dog
it is not where we were told to look. Not curled
on his roof. Not barking from the glassless window
of his attic. When we find Clausen's dog it is tied
to a cinderblock with a choke-chain leash,
an ear-flap lapping softly at the surface.
The choke-chain cinches down through loose
neck-flesh to the visible bone. A minnow hovers
in the eye-hole. When we find Clausen's dog
the colorless fur clumps like a stubble of bunchgrass
receding from the furrowed plains of the rib cage.
The bobbing sidemeat nibbled by perch.
Chunks glaumed away by turtles.
When we find Clausen's dog the bone-paws drag
the bottom like lures, jerking forward
on the same wrist-hinge as the living paws
of a sleeping dog, whimpering, trying to run
inside a dream.

ICEFISHER

The man sets the fish house far out
on the lake. Drills the hole.
Scoops the slush out with a ladle.
Silence and the lake and the man.
The pine hills folded in fog,
faded to ash and gunpowder.
The maple leaves fallen and lost
in the snow. The gray ghost
thin and sinewy, moving off through
the coal-black remnants of branches.
If you cannot see it in winter
you will never see it.
The man goes into the dark house
and lowers his lure. The deep hole
glows. The water is clear.
The low hoot of the owl simmers
the shore meridian as evening
comes on and the hole
darkens. He breathes into his hands.
He lets out a little more line.

LIVING

I get everything I need for free.
These boots came from the factory
dumpster on the far side of town. This hat
was moldering on the kitchen floor
in the foreclosed home I picked through.
This coat, this backpack, this brand-
name headlamp. I got this cornmeal
behind the grocery store, this flatbread
behind the bakery, this french press
in the alleyway next to the coffee shop in uptown.
This bible in a bum camp, this banjo
in a trash can, this headless mannequin
in a free-pile outside Honest Ed's Antiques.
The British call it skipping.
The Brazilians call it living, call it vida.
Vida que surgi de nada. Life out of nothing.
I bike past the butcher's on Pike
and find a bag full of pigs.
None of them whole. A few sets of hooves,
a half torso, two heads, another head
with no nose, a leg, a pile of coiled tails
slowly uncoiling like white worms
taken out of a hole. Most of it
going musty, the muscle falling away
from the fascia, the skin drained of color
and feeling like withered pumpkin.
But some of it might be good.
A pair of milky gloves is clumped up
and tangled among the little hairless tails.
I dig them out. I blow to check
for holes. I begin sorting the pigs.

FLOOD OF '97

In the flood of '97 everything went to shit.
Somewhere in Canada the Red River clogged
and coated the roads in downtown Fargo
as high as the stop signs. Not much was saved.
Dark water churned for a moment as the river
tipped over, then a stillness filled the basements.
It was the same all over town. The rambler rooftops
looming like islands. Foundations rotting
in the afternoon silence. Everybody camping
in a cousin's backyard, or staying with an uncle
down in Fergus. The old folks at Eventide
had to move to Oak Grove and spent two weeks
sleeping on cots in the brick chapel.
When the ice sheets broke and the brown water
flowed up to Hudson Bay, the basements drained
and people opened their own front doors
like strangers. Tiptoed through bedrooms
and ran their hands over water-warped walls.
Went in the kitchen and swore the fridge
had been moved. All summer, people found
rusty things they didn't recognize, things
that must have floated in from other homes.
Fathers walked the silty streets and knocked
on doors, trying to find the rightful owner
of a shovel or a broom. An elderly woman returned
to Eventide and discovered a soggy photograph
on the mildewed carpet in her tiny room.
She peered at the blurry faces and tried to remember
going to Egypt. Wondered who the man could be,
standing beside her at the Sphinx.

TO THE FINGERLESS MAN IN BANFF

There was little you couldn't do.
With the purple stump of your thumb
you pinned a pencil against
the knuckle-lumps, forming enough grip
to sketch her portrait from memory,
or from the photo you kept hid
in your hatband. You worked the ranches
like before. Rode horses. Knotted
ropes. Shuffled when you dealt.
You let me ball old newsprint
for the fire, but you did everything else.
Gutted the fish. Stuffed the belly
with berries and butter and smoked it
by rotating a willow stick.
And when you folded your hands
to whisper the words over the meal,
nothing folded, but what kind of world
would this be if that mattered?
Your cheeks filled and flickered
as you chewed. The embers bedded down
and the clouds born out of them
twisted through the cottonwoods.
You never told me her name.
That could jinx it, you said.
*If I find her again it ain't gonna be
as a detective.* You could even roll
your own cigarettes, but you couldn't
roll the striker on a Bic.
I flicked it alive for you. Your palms
pulled my hand toward your lips.

THE RAFT

He baits the hook with an Indian Paintbrush petal,
lets out the line, reels, traps it with his thumb-pad.
October. Powder on the peaks. We float on a raft
lashed together with a loose weave of duct-tape and rope.
I paddle us forward with a cottonwood branch,
my leg in the water for a rudder, trying to hold us close
to the darkness of the drop-off where the trout go
to stay cool in the afternoons. Later we'll make a fire
and cook our catch with blueberries gathered frozen
from the cirque above the tarn. We'll blow on the coals.
We'll check for tenderness. We'll add ash in place
of salt. But for now I'm watching the sunlight
bounce off the surface and shimmer in the shadow
under my brother's hat. The way he plays the line.
The way he lets it troll behind us. The way the trout
cloud our wake and flick their rainbowed sides.
I'm torquing my leg underwater. I'm turning us back
toward the darkness we've drifted away from.

COUNTY 19

for Elizabeth Day Wee

I twist in my seat beside the woman who picked me up
on County 19, reaching back to help her son
eat his Happy Meal. I fly a french fry through the air,
thinking how weird it is to hitch a ride on the road
I've driven so many times with my dad—
the route between our house and the old folks home
where Grandma lasted alone for fourteen years.
Each time we visited: the veins wider, bluer,
the ankles thinner, the distances between bedsores
diminished, the cheer my dad convinced himself to feel
as he repeated the litany: *I am your son.*
This is your grandson. We are so happy to see you.
The woman asks me where I'm going
and I say as far as you can take me,
but as we pass the old folks home I tell her to pull over.
The boy is finished with his Happy Meal
and now he points at the bruise on his elbow and says *Ouch.*
His mom nods at him in the rearview as I get out.
That's right, she says. *Ouch.* There is the low roofline,
the sign with a bible quote in changeable letters,
my grandma's old window as blank as it was
when she lived here, some earth dug up
in the bordering cornfield for construction
of a new wing. I think about barging through the doors,
demanding to see Elizabeth Wee,
making some kind of scene. I think about setting up camp
in the hole in the cornfield, refusing to leave.
But instead I wander around the grounds for awhile.
I lie in the parking lot's grass island,
the cornstalks feathering the road with lank shadows,

the sunlight dipping down into the tassels.
In the twilight I walk back to the shoulder
and take a ride from a farmer hauling a trailer
stacked with hay bales three-high. When he asks me
where I'm going I say as far as you can take me.

GATHERING FIREWOOD ON TINPAN

I bundle them against my chest, not sure
if they're dry enough. Gauging how long
they'll keep me warm by the thickness.
I step around carefully, looking for the deadest,
searching the low places
for something small and old that will catch.
I pick up the dander loosened
as my father folds his hands, lowers his head.
The rolling thunder on the surface of a nail.
I pick up the cross that seesaws his chest
with each step. The day I lost my faith.
The night my dog ran away and came back sick.
The battery-pump of her final breath.
Still wondering if she left alone,
or if my father walked her out of this world.
Still wondering what he used for a leash.
I go further into the trees and find
more fuel. My friends faded on oxy
and percocet. My cousin Scott
buried young in the floodplain.
My brother and the ways I burden him.
Living it over and over each night.
My father walking into every dream.
My fire not bright enough to reveal anything.
Not even his face. Not even the leash.

MOORCROFT

You gave me a ride when I was lost
in Wyoming. Took me to your home.
Showed me your gun collection
you had to go shoulder-deep
through the clothes in the closet to reach.
They were old and unloaded,
you told me, and you didn't shoot them
anymore, just oiled them and kept them
perfectly clean. I was careful not to flinch
as I watched the double-barrel
raise and train on my face.
The tooth-hole you flashed
in the grin after. The spasm in your hands
as you swung the gun and pointed it
at yourself to show evenness.
You told me about doing five years
for murder, asked if I would've done
anything different, finding a grown man
raping my six-year-old niece.
I wouldn't change it, you said.
I wouldn't take it back. You patted
your heart with your hand.
Family is family, you whispered,
as you brought me clean sheets for my bed.

POLAROID

A loose flap of skin passes just below
his eye. Bruises ride the bridge of my nose.
The dark ropes of handprints grip
both our necks. Our fresh buzz-cuts
lumpy with goose eggs. It's easy to forget
we were trying to kill each other.
Or at least I was. But what I wonder now
is why our father shot the photo before
he bandaged the hole where the nail
went in, stuffed my raw mouth with gauze.
We stand side by side against the garage,
eyes focused just beyond the lens,
each pointing at what we did to the other.

SHOALWATER

Waves grind the shoreline and darken into pools.
Crabs shuffle sideways, lost in the washed-up eelgrass.
Seagulls spit littleneck clams to the rocks
and don't even eat the shattered bodies.
They fly as high as the clouds and wrap talons
in the wind. But this kind of love isn't rare.
When I dream about my brother he disappears
if I look. He wears a bird-bone bracelet,
but I only know this by feel. Even his hair
is something I imagine. His nose occurs solely
as contours. I walk down the beach
and throw stones at the oncoming waves.
This is the best we can do. We leak every time
we are opened. Out just beyond the waves,
love says the same of itself. We can only witness
the implication, only feel for the shape.
Love is a pigeon nestled beside a dead pigeon
at night in the wet corner of a warehouse.
Blackness and the texture of feathers.
The thud of a body surrounded by hollow.
Love is a clamshell's first touch against rock,
whatever tenderness can be found
in that contact before the crack. It's been years
since I was last out on the water. The night sky tightens
like that familiar mouth. Clouds hide their bulk
on the backsides of islands. Each wave is real
the way his body is real. Made of something
not itself. Something bigger. Call it water.
Call it wind. Call it tendon-flexing of the moon.
Each wave lifts as he lifts, crashes as he crashes.
Love exists in the way seagulls hold still
in the wind. The way crabs carry pieces of clam
through the moonlight and vanish sideways into sand.

BUTTE

My brother bolt-cuts a hole through the mesh
over the Family Dollar dumpster in Butte.
I lower myself through. Dull light mumbles
from the car-emptied lot, slumping
on day-old donuts, moldy seed bread,
a bulk-bag of oats the rats have chewed through.
I hand up the bread. I hand up the donuts.
I hand up the tub of yogurt someone
bought, opened, tasted, and returned.
I go shoulder-deep through the yolk-crusted bags,
reaching—maybe fruit, maybe meat.
After awhile you can name what you feel.
Groping wet shapes with the tips of your fingers.
Lifting them up to your brother.

THE LOW PASSIONS

The Lord came down because God wasn't enough.
He lies on sodden cardboard behind bushes
in the churchyard. Wrapped in faded red. A sleeping bag
he found or traded for. Dark stains like clouds
before a downpour. The stone wall beside him rising,
always rising, the edges of stone going blunt
where the choirboy climbs. He opens his mouth,
but nothing goes in and nothing comes out.
Like the sideshow man who long ago lost
his right testicle to the crossbar of a Huffy.
He peddles the leftover pain. The stitches clipped
a week later by his father, the fiberglass bathtub
running with color, the puffy new scar,
the crooked look of the pitted half-sack.
He tells me you only need one nut, and I want
to believe him. I want to believe he can still
get it up. I want to believe he has daughters, sons,
a grandchild on the way, a wife at home
in a blue apron baking. But why this day-old bread
from the dumpster, this stash of hollow bottles
in the buckthorn, this wrinkled can of Pabst?
The Lord came down because God wasn't enough.
Because the childless man draws the bathwater
and cries. Because the choirboy never sings
as he climbs. Because the bread has all molded
and the mouths are all open. Open to the clotting air.
Homeless, anything helps. Anything. Anything you can
spare. God bless you, God bless you, God bless. God,
Lord God, God God, good God, good Lord very good God.

LISTENING TO A RAIL IN MANDAN

I've heard it said that you can feel it coming
in the tremor of the tracks, that you can cock
your head and cup an ear to the smooth steel
and sense it coming in vibrations, in rattles,
that you can gather the blaze of friction
as it builds, the heart murmur climbing the pass
through the mountains inside your head.
I stand at the edge of the brake and listen
for far-off signs: whistles, footfalls, gravel
ground under truck tires. I crawl up the grade
to the raised beds and the rails, the bull-run
on the far side of the yard lit by overheads,
each pool of light like a crude betrayal
of the darknesses between. The rails
take parallel trails of light past the sidings,
past the curve at the end of the yard,
past the bottleneck at the Heart River bridge—
two aisles of light like childhood brothers adrift,
like a father's eyes carving the dark land
beside the dark river. The shape of a tree.
The shape of an owl grinding the sky.
I've heard it said that you can feel it coming
from as far off as a mile, the distance erased
in the pump of a vein, in the flicker of overhead lights,
the bull-run laying in its own dust wasted,
the tire tracks zigzagged and stacked
where the rail-cop makes fate his listless routine.
I shoulder against a fishplate and lower
my head to the rail. I wait for a chime, a shiver,
some thunder to ride past the overland silence.
I've heard it said that the kingdom of heaven

surrounds us, though we fail to see.
No stars tonight. No fire. No brother by the junkers
awaiting my call. No father walking toward me
on the tar-blackened ties. No dog's eye
catching the searchlights. Not a single sound
fleshing this tank town as the rail begins to shake,
as the train begins to whisper my name.

GLOSSARY OF TERMS

— *Bull*

Railroad police officer.

— *Bull Run*

Road patrolled by railroad police in a train yard.

— *Gray Ghost*

Nickname for the Great Gray Owl.

— *Owl's Eye*

Circular hole on the porch of a Canadian Grainer train car, in which a train-hopper can ride in concealment.

ABOUT THE AUTHOR

ANDERS CARLSON-WEE is a 2015 NEA Fellow and
2015 Bread Loaf Bakeless Camargo Fellow. His work
has appeared in *Narrative, New England Review,
The Missouri Review, The Southern Review, Blackbird,
Best New Poets,* and *The Best American Nonrequired
Reading* series. Winner of *Ninth Letter*'s Poetry Award
and *New Delta Review*'s Editors' Choice Prize, he
holds an MFA in poetry from Vanderbilt University.

About

THE FROST PLACE CHAPBOOK COMPETITION

The Frost Place is a nonprofit educational center for poetry and the arts based at Robert Frost's old homestead, which is owned by the Town of Franconia, New Hampshire. In 1976, a group of Franconia residents, led by David Schaffer and Evangeline Machlin, persuaded the Franconia town meeting to approve the purchase of the farmhouse where Robert Frost and his family lived full-time from 1915 to 1920 and spent nineteen summers. A board of trustees was given responsibility for management of the house and its associated programs, which now include several conferences and seminars, readings, a museum located in the Frost farmhouse, and yearly fellowships for emerging American poets.

The Frost Place Chapbook Competition awards an annual prize to a chapbook of poems. In addition to publication of the collection by Bull City Press, the winning author receives a fellowship to The Frost Place Poetry Seminar, a cash prize, and week-long residency to live and write in The Frost Place farmhouse.

2015   Anders Carlson-Wee, *Dynamite*
SELECTED BY JENNIFER GROTZ

2014   Lisa Gluskin Stonestreet, *The Greenhouse*
SELECTED BY DAVID BAKER

2013   Jill Osier, *Should Our Undoing Come Down Upon Us White*
SELECTED BY PATRICK DONNELLY

ALSO FROM BULL CITY PRESS

KATIE BOWLER
State Street

ELLEN C. BUSH
Licorice

ANNE KEEFE
Lithopedia

MICHAEL McFEE
The Smallest Talk

EMILIA PHILLIPS
Beneath the Ice Fish Like Souls Look Alike

MATTHEW OLZMANN & ROSS WHITE, eds.
Another & Another:
An Anthology from the Grind Daily Writing Series